AIR UNIVERSITY

Air Force Research Institute
Perspectives on Cyber Power

Social Media

The Fastest Growing Vulnerability to the Air Force Mission

Scott E. Solomon
Lieutenant Colonel, USAF

CPP–6

Project Editor
James S. Howard

Copy Editor
Carolyn B. Underwood

Cover Art, Book Design, and Illustrations
Daniel Armstrong

Composition and Prepress Production
Vivian D. O'Neal

Print Preparation and Distribution
Diane Clark

Director and Publisher
Dale L. Hayden, PhD

Editor in Chief
Oreste M. Johnson

Managing Editor
Dr. Ernest Allan Rockwell

Design and Production Manager
Cheryl King

ISBN: 978-1973751281

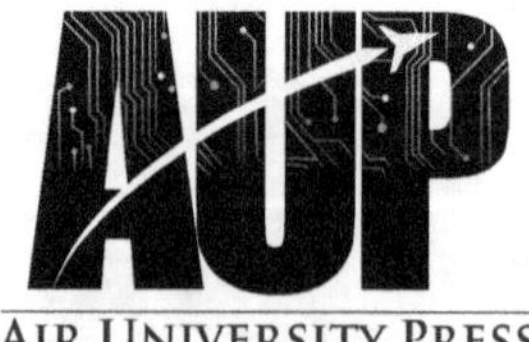

Disclaimer

Opinions, conclusions, and recommendations expressed or implied within are solely those of the author and do not necessarily repre-sent the views of the Air Force Research Institute, Air University, the United States Air Force, the Department of Defense, or any other US government agency.

Air Force Research Institute Perspectives on Cyber Power

We live in a world where global efforts to provide access to cyber resources and the battles for control of cyberspace are intensifying. In this series, leading international experts explore key topics on cyber disputes and collaboration. Written by practitioners and renowned scholars who are leaders in their fields, the publications provide original and accessible overviews of subjects about cyber power, conflict, and cooperation.

As a venue for dialogue and study about cyber power and its relationship to national security, military operations, economic policy, and other strategic issues, this series aims to provide essential reading for senior military leaders, professional military education students, and interagency, academic, and private-sector partners. These intellectually rigorous studies draw on a range of contemporary examples and contextualize their subjects within the broader defense and diplomacy landscapes.

These and other Air Force Research Institute studies are available via the AU Press website at http://aupress.au.af.mil/papers.asp. Please submit comments to afri.public@maxwell.af.mil.

Contents

List of Illustrations

About the Author

Lt Col Scott E. Solomon is assigned to the Air War College, Air University, Maxwell AFB, AL. Colonel Solomon is a career cyberspace operations officer. Born and raised in Southern California, he enlisted in the Air Force in 1988 as a precision measurement equipment laboratory specialist. In 1993, he completed Officer Training School and became a communications and information systems engineering officer. His assignments include various cyberspace, space and airborne operational assignments, and various staff and engineering support positions in six major commands including the Air Staff. In 2006, he served as the joint forces air component commander's command and control planner directly supporting Operation Iraqi Freedom and Operation Enduring Freedom. He has commanded a squadron and served as a deputy group commander. In his prior assignment, Colonel Solomon was the executive officer to the vice commander, Air Education and Training Command.

Abstract

Social media is the fastest growing vulnerability to the military mission and the personal security of all Airmen. On 30 November 2014, the FBI issued warning to members of the US military and requested that they review their social media presence for any information like names and addresses that might attract the attention of violent ISIS extremists.[1] Over the past decade, the convergence of mobile broadband devices has enabled social media to become more and more integrated into our everyday lives. The inherent risks and vulnerabilities of the internet and social networking sites like Facebook, LinkedIn, and Twitter along with the Air Force's endorsement to actively use social media, has cultivated a rich and ripe environment for foreign adversaries and criminals to cherry-pick personal information about Airmen and their missions for nefarious activities. To help Americans understand the risks that come with being online, the Department of Homeland Security launched a new cybersecurity awareness campaign: Stop, Think, and Connect.[2] To educate Airmen on social media, AF public affairs created the "Air Force Social Media Guide" in 2013 to encourage Airmen to share their AF experiences with family and friends in the social media environment. However, this is counter to the FBI's guidance that promotes the reduction of users' on-line footprint and online presence in cyberspace.[3]

Notes

(All notes appear in shortened form. For full details, see the appropriate entry in the bibliography.)

1. Brown and Sciutto, "FBI warn military of ISIS threat."
2. DHS, "Stop, Think, Connect."
3. FBI, "Internet Social Networking Risks."

Chapter 1

The Problem

Social media is the fastest growing vulnerability to the military mission and the personal security of all Airmen. In the networked world of desktop and mobile devices, the lines between official work and the personal use of social media are getting harder to define. On 30 November 2014, the Federal Bureau of Investigation (FBI) issued a warning to members of the US military and requested that they review their social media presence for any personal information like names and addresses that might attract the attention of violent Islamic State of Iraq and Syria (ISIS) extremists.[1] Over the past decade, the convergence of mobile broadband devices has enabled social media to become more integrated into our everyday lives. Additionally, specific social media sites such as Facebook, LinkedIn, and E-Harmony continue to shape and influence the way we engage with others socially, for professional networking, and options for dating. The inherent risks and vulnerabilities of the internet and social networking sites, taken with the Air Force's endorsing the active use of social media, has cultivated a rich and ripe environment for foreign adversaries and criminals to cherry-pick personal information about Airmen and their missions for nefarious activities.

Public Affairs published the "Air Force Social Media Guide" in 2013 to encourage Airmen to share their Air Force experiences with family and friends in the social media environment with the following introduction: "This guide will help you share information effectively while following Air Force instructions and protecting operations security."[2] The guide does an excellent job identifying the "shoulds" and "should nots" in social media; however, the guide does not address hardware vulnerabilities or the risks of using social media sites. This paper will respond to some of the most common threats and vulnerabilities of the social media environment, the risks of using social media, and the current Air Force social media guidance. It will also provide recommendations to educate better and inform Airmen and their families on using social media sites and cyberspace best practices.

Notes

(All notes appear in shortened form. For full details, see the appropriate entry in the bibliography.)

1. Brown and Sciutto, "FBI Warn Military of ISIS Threat."
2. Air Force Public Affairs Agency. *Air Force Social Media Guide*, 2.

Chapter 2

Threats and Vulnerabilities—What Is Different from the Past?

Today's cyberspace environment provides an engaging interactive experience for social networking, picture and video sharing, and blogs that keep end users engaged and wanting to share or consume more information. In addition to social media sites, commercial web services, online commerce services, and the hardware used for networking can provide the means to compromise sensitive information. Threats to desktop computer hardware are important but fall outside the scope of this paper; an example is in the notes.[1] Today's hackers have discovered exquisite ways to install malware on a user's computer hardware through seemingly innocuous means by exploiting security breaches in social media websites that use Java, Ajax, or other popular software technologies. Opening up files or hyperlinks attached to social media messages or email attachments may contain malware that can bypass firewalls or virus protection programs. In many cases, this happens without the user knowing they have become a victim or that their hardware is infected.[2]

Department of Defense (DOD) members are attractive targets for foreign adversaries and criminals using sophisticated scams and fraud schemes designed to take advantage of the unsuspecting users to extort information or money. One of the techniques used by malicious actors is to create fictitious online personas on popular social media sites and attempt to send "friend" or "connect" requests to potential targets.[3] Unlike traditional spear-phishing emails with malicious attachments or hyperlinks that try to get unsuspecting victims to execute the attachment, accepting a "friend" or "connect" request adds a personal social touch to the process where the victim believes they have a personal connection with whoever sent the requests. This technique conditions the victim into thinking that whomever they connect to is a legitimate friend or a friend of a friend. As social media friends, these malicious actors often attempt to make direct contact with the victim to solicit additional personal information for financial gain, identity theft, or information to compromise the mission.

Before the advent of smartphones and social media platforms, the predominant vulnerability for compromising privacy in cyberspace was hacking the home computer. In 1988, the first computer worm referred to as the "Morris Worm," hit the internet and infected one out of every 20 computers.[4] Since that time, bad actors have developed techniques that take advantage of built-in hardware and software vulnerabilities to compromise personal data and steal information. Additionally, as more people started using personal computers, hardware theft, careless password security practices, surfing infected websites, and overall poor security practices made the job of stealing information easier for criminal actors. Over time, firewalls and virus protection software closed some of the vulnerabilities in home and business computers. Additionally, user education, automatic software updates, and better password management processes made stealing information harder for criminals. Fast forward to the present, the proliferation of mobile devices used for sharing personal information on social media networks has provided bad actors new opportunities to infect hardware with malware that can take over computer functions or divulge personal information.

Mobile Device Vulnerabilities

Accessing social media is today's number one mobile activity. Of those surveyed, 71 percent use their mobile phone to access social media.[5] Today's mobile devices are extremely capable minicomputers that can give users much of the same functionality as their home computer while providing portable capabilities that can enhance or provide productivity while on the go. Due to the proliferation of mobile devices, many folks spend more time processing information on their mobile devices than they do at home. In fact, internet usage on mobile devices exceeded personal computer usage for the first time in early 2014.[6] Functionality and productivity achieved with the use of embedded or downloadable apps have created another vulnerability that marketing firms and malicious actors can use to track an individual's location, consume personal information, or add malware to a device for future exploitation. In the last example, once access is established with malware, it can be hard to detect and clean before any information is compromised.

Vulnerabilities of Free Apps

Symantec's latest "2013 Internet Security Threat Report" stated that information stealing is the top threat from mobile malware or overly aggressive ad networks.[7] Free apps and embedded social media programs that come preloaded on mobile devices may be appealing to use, but they may be placing personal information at risk. Some of the free apps out there may not cost real money but can cost in terms of time spent getting past nuisance ads, limited program functionality, or exposing personal information to third party vendors. The most common examples are as follows:

- The developer gets paid for providing banner advertising for other products.
- The developer limits the functionality or features of the app.

In these cases, a small fee is required to remove the advertising or to activate a full functioning product. The other common practice for a free app is to grant the program elevated permissions to view personal information, discover accounts, read contacts, and even read text messages. Before installing a free app, it is important to note that the app may have elevated permissions that can enable information collection activities.

One of the keys to protecting one's information is to understand what permissions the app may need to do its job before installing it. As more and more families use mobile devices with social media apps to stay in touch with deployed family members and friends, they may be unknowingly putting personal information at risk. In 2003, three Estonian programmers located in Sweden created the popular video chat software application called "Skype."[8] It was an instant hit in the United States and abroad which brought video chat capability to the home computer. With the advent of smartphones, this created an opportunity to provide a free mobile app in return for some elevated permissions. The latest Skype app acquires permissions to read text messages, storage contents, and an extensive list of other items that provide personal information. Skype's privacy policy states that they can collect, analyze, and provide third-party service providers with personal data, messages, and passwords under the guise of "providing you with a safe, smooth, efficient, and customized experience." Before installing an app, evaluate the risk by reading the developer's privacy policy and permission details.

Bring Your Own Device Program

To add another vulnerability to the mix, the White House Federal chief information officer put out the "Digital Government Strategy" in 2012 on its new Bring Your Own Device (BYOD) program for government agencies so you can use your personal device for official work. This new strategy opened the door for government agencies to explore the reality of allowing employees to use personal computer or mobile devices for official work. The US Equal Employment Opportunity Commission ran one of the first pilot programs using personal mobile devices for official work. The pilot showed favorable user results and reduced overall operational costs for the organization.[9] Many government agencies are moving forward to take advantage of the BYOD program.

The Air Force is also working towards a mobile device rollout plan that will allow its members to use government email and applications on their personal devices for official work. To ensure mobile device data security requirements are operationalized, the Air Force teamed up with "Good Technology" to provide a software solution that keeps official data separate and secure by using a secure software container approach to store information on the device.[10] This software add-on enables the use of official email and other work applications on a personal device while retaining the ability to access personal applications. While protecting data through security is a top concern for most organizations, there are many more factors to consider for a successful BYOD program rollout as shown in figure 1 below.[11] Regardless of how well the Air Force deploys BYOD to Airmen, software add-ons will not be a panacea for mitigating the vulnerabilities or risk of storing official data on personal devices.

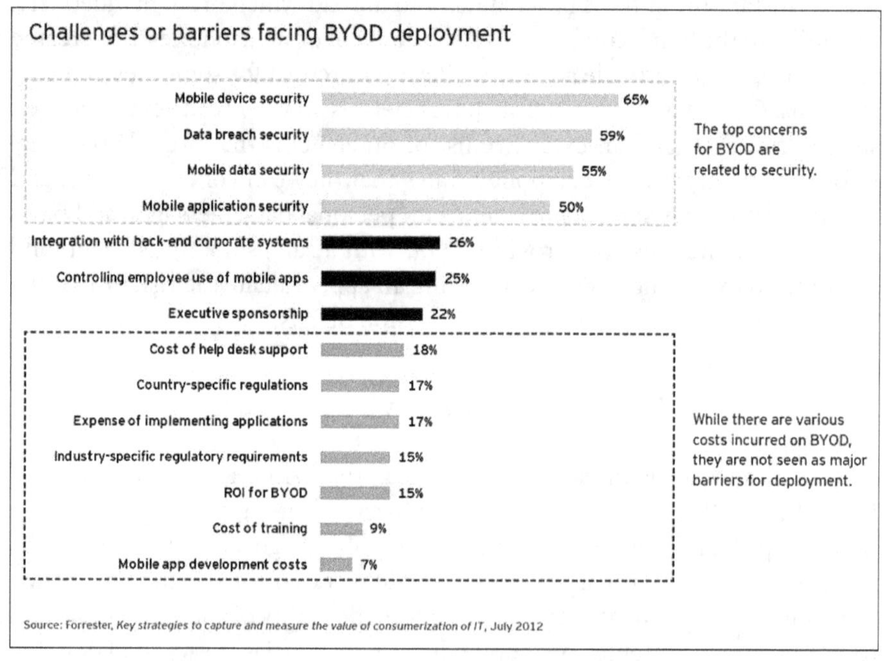

Figure 1. Top industry BYOD concerns (Reprinted from Forrester Consulting, "Key Strategies to Capture and Measure the Consumerization of IT.")

When evaluating the risk and vulnerabilities of storing official information on personal devices, the current statistical research infers that the risk of exposing "For Official Use Only" or privacy act information will increase. Pew Research Center studies show approximately 22 percent of the total number of mobile devices will be lost or stolen during their lifetime with only 50 percent recovered intact. A growing number of these stolen devices purposely have their content accessed by someone other than the owners.[12] Accordingly, as more and more people use the BYOD program for work, the risk of exposing official information will climb due to the physical loss or theft of devices. Therefore, while the BYOD program may reduce the overall operating cost for the government and provide convenience to the end user, encrypting data, user education, and strong mobile security are key to protecting the information. As new vulnerabilities are regularly discovered, user education and the process of securing information networks and systems must be continuous and timely.

Notes

1. Authors Note: On 15 August 2012, a malicious virus allegedly developed by Iran attacked the Saudi oil company Aramco that resulted in erased documents, spreadsheets, emails, and files on over 30,000 corporate PCs. The attack shut down major operations and took 11 days to restore the computers back to normal operations. In some cases, malware has sat idle and undetected for years until the virus is discovered and a virus signature is deployed that can clean the malware from the system. Malicious actors have the ability to tailor malware to an individual or an entire organization. Once malware establishes a foothold in the system, the limits to what it can do in the background are bounded only by the programmer knowledge of the target. This can include taking pictures or video with a webcam device, capturing the keystrokes on a keyboard for username and password collection, or downloading the information that resides on a hard drive or server. Higgins, "30,000 Machines Infected."
2. Oxley, "Best Practices Guide," 20, 22.
3. Air Force Office of Special Investigations (AFOSI), *AFOSI Special Product*, 2, 8.
4. Oman, "The Morris Worm," 34.
5. Pun, "Adobe 2013 Mobile Consumer Survey."
6. Murtagh, "Mobile Now Exceeds PC."
7. Gonsalves, "Eight Tips."
8. Thomann, "Skype."
9. White House, "Bring Your Own Device," 8.
10. Reynolds, "Good Technology Supports Air Force."
11. Ernst and Young Global, Limited, *Bring Your Own Device*, 2.
12. Ibid., 4.

Chapter 3

Using Social Media—What is the Risk?

The social media risk to the mission and the personal security of Airmen and their families is real and on the rise. On 7 October 2014, as reported by Fox News, an Army intelligence bulletin warned its members that ISIS militants were calling on supporters to scour social media network and profiles for the addresses of US military family members and to "show up at their homes and slaughter them."[1] In another case, Islamic State sympathizers targeted the Facebook pages of an Air Force father and son after a series of pictures of a recent Iraq bombing campaign were posted on a military website. The sympathizers tracked the pictures to the members' Facebook sites and proceeded to swarm them with offensive messages and threats.[2] These two examples demonstrate the increasing risk of posting information in cyberspace and demonstrate the power of exploiting social media information for criminal activity. Despite the warnings in the news and stories of personal information theft, the level of social media engagement continues to increase as shown in figure 2 below.[3]

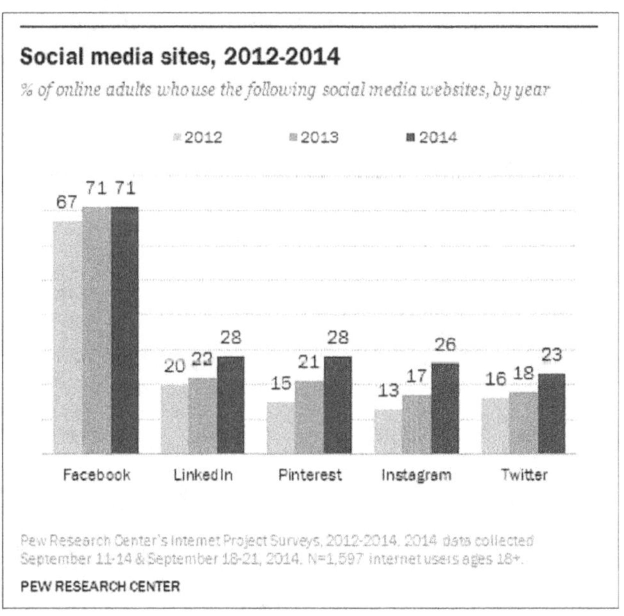

Figure 2. Top social media site trends (Reprinted from Duggan et al., "Social Media Update 2014.")

Trends in Targeting Personal Information

A recent article on "Are Your Facebook Posts Compromising Military Security" suggests that you need to think very carefully about everything that you post on the internet; once posted, most anyone can access it, and it is out there forever.[4] The classic Facebook example is to use profile and newsfeed information to find potential victims in the vicinity that will not be home, or are on vacation, to make it easier for the criminals to break into the house.[5] Also, personal information stored in data repositories, financial institutions, and third party vendors provide an additional vulnerability for data aggregators to exploit. According to the 2014 Mandiant report on cyberspace security, the list of potential cyber targets has increased over the years and continues to grow. From 2013 to 2014, cyber threat activities increased 4 percent for financial services and a 6 percent in the media and entertainment sector. Another trend they noticed was 44 percent of the phishing emails sent were information technology related in hopes of getting the end user to reply or click on the link that can download malware or redirect the user to an infected web page. Also, 93 percent of the phishing emails were sent to potential victims during the week with the highest volume occurring on Wednesdays. However, as shown in figure 3 below, one of the most alarming trends identified in the report is how long it can take to discover that a compromise occurred.[6] For the uninformed user, cyberspace can be a dangerous place where posting information or surfing the internet can make them a target of opportunity.

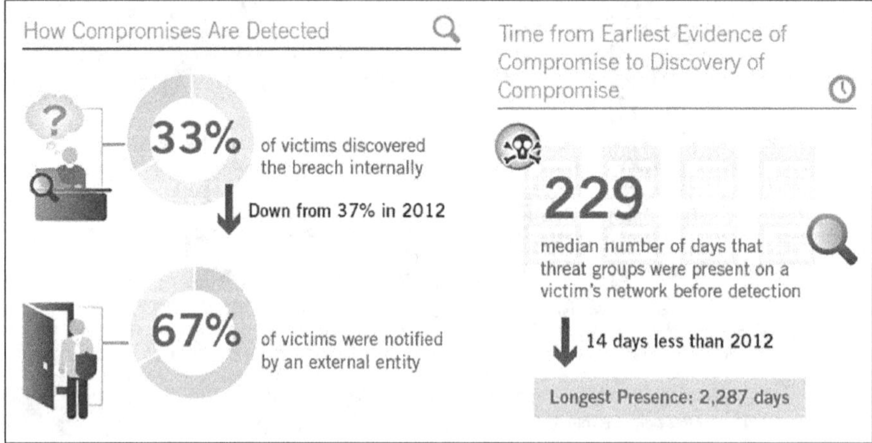

Figure 3. The amount of time it can take to discover a compromise (Reprinted from M-Trends, "Mandiant Annual Threat Report—2014: Beyond the Breach.")

Data Mining Personal Information

A recent Air Force Office of Special Investigations report on "Safeguarding USAF Personnel's Online Presence" suggests that DOD members need to be vigilant about posting personal information on social networking sites such as Facebook and LinkedIn for possible fraud and solicitation schemes.[7] Information posted to these sites can be harvested and correlated by others using data mining tools. LinkedIn is a valuable source of business networking information and can be utilized as a way of enumerating networks of individuals at a micro and macro scale. By exploiting profile information and the linkages provided by connections made by individual users, it is possible to map an individual's interests, their network of contacts, or an entire organization.[8]

Personal information, newspaper archives, court records, and even simple Google searches provide a vast amount of information freely available that can be cross-referenced and filtered to provide insightful intelligence.[9] For example, pictures use an exchangeable image file format (EXIF) standard to store image information. When these files are uploaded to social media sites, bad actors can use software that can read the embedded image information and provide geolocation information about the picture.[10] Maltego is another extremely powerful open-source intelligence data aggregator platform that can gather and correlate vast amounts of information found on the internet or social media sites. Figure 4 on the next page is a screenshot of Maltego mapping of connections showing how the tool can correlate specific connections.[11] These two software tools that anyone can use are just a few of the many online tools available to harvest person-specific information such as social networking activity, email addresses, or websites associated with the user.[12] This information can be used for marketing, crime, or foreign adversaries looking for hacking or social engineering targets of opportunity.

Perceptions of Social Media Risk

Internalizing the impact of the real threat to a member's personal security or the mission is a matter of where one sits, how much one engages with social media, and the results of one's past online experiences. A recent US Gallup poll on households victimized by crime stated that 27 percent of households and 19 percent of US adults say they have been affected by stolen credit card information in the past 12 months. Meanwhile, 11 percent of households and 7 percent of Americans say they had a computer or a smartphone hacked and information stolen by unauthorized users. According to Gallup, if the newer cyber crimes of credit card theft and computer hacking were included in the statistics, the household victimization rate would surge to 46 percent (up from 26 percent), and the individual victimization rate would jump to 34 percent (up from 19 percent).[13] It is important to note that these figures are only for adults and for those adults that know their information was compromised. Most people have a false sense of security because, as far as they are aware, they have not been a victim of identity theft, fraud, or data exfiltration. Also, a large majority of Airmen believes their online practices are relatively safe at work and home; otherwise, the DOD would not have opened up the dot-mil network for social media and other web service activities that they can do at their desk.

Figure 4. Maltego connection mapping (Created by James Alexander using Maltego CaseFile software, Jalexander-WMF at English Wikipedia.)

Due to people's proclivity for posting personal information on the internet and social media sites, bad actors have many opportunities to construct concise victim profiles for targeted attacks. Public perceptions of privacy and security after classified information leaks by NSA contractor Edward Snowden reveal a universal lack of confidence among adults in the safety of normal communications channels as shown in figure 5 below. Whereas before this event, users felt more comfortable that their posts were secure and confined within the environment they created regarding friends or connections. However, among adults surveyed, 59 percent have posted comments or questions using a user name or screen name that people can associate with them, and more than 50 percent have done so using their real name.[14] Although research suggests context matters as people decide whether to disclose personal information online, it also shows that users tend to bounce back and forth between different levels of disclosure depending on the context and their sense of security.[16] In summary, the use of social media sites continues to grow even though the research shows people are a little more cautious than they were in the past about posting information online.

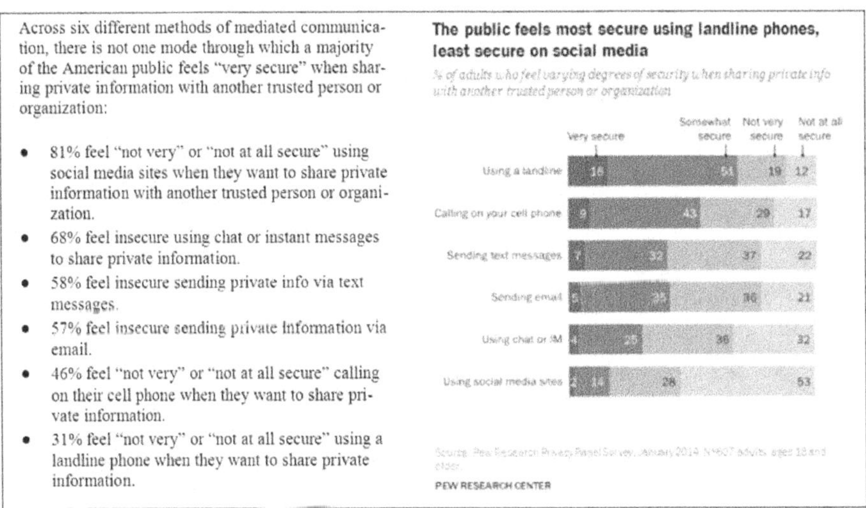

- 81% feel "not very" or "not at all secure" using social media sites when they want to share private information with another trusted person or organization.
- 68% feel insecure using chat or instant messages to share private information.
- 58% feel insecure sending private info via text messages.
- 57% feel insecure sending private information via email.
- 46% feel "not very" or "not at all secure" calling on their cell phone when they want to share private information.
- 31% feel "not very" or "not at all secure" using a landline phone when they want to share private information.

Figure 5. Public perceptions of information security (Reprinted from Madden, "Privacy and Cybersecurity.")

Notes

1. Herridge, "Source: Air Force Father, Son Targeted."
2. Ibid.
3. Duggan et al., "Social Media Update 2014."
4. Schelihaas, "Are Your Facebook Posts Compromising?"

5. Boone, "Criminal Use of Social Media," 1.

6. *M-Trends: Beyond the Breach: Mandiant Annual Threat Report—2014*, 2–3.

7. AFOSI, *AFOSI Special Product*.

8. Bradbury, "Data Mining."

9. Bradbury, "In Plain View."

10. Opanda, "Power EXIF® Editor."

11. Alexander, "Maltego Connection Mapping."

12. Paterva, "Maltego Software."

13. Jones, "About One in Four US Households Victimized by Crime."

14. Ibid.

15. Madden, "Public Perceptions of Privacy and Security."

Chapter 4

Air Force Social Media
Guidance—What's Missing?

In 2010, the DOD authorized the services and its members to use the dot-mil domain and infrastructure to access social media sites. However, educating the workforce concerning the risks and vulnerabilities of using social media has been challenging. Under the current policy, Airmen can use their government computer for accessing social media sites and commercial emails services while at work as long as it does not interfere with mission related duties. Air Force members can also access government webmail accounts using their computer at home or on the road for accomplishing official government work. This change in policy provides the user with more flexibility but also increases the risk to the network. For example, a mobile computer could be compromised with malware that could make its way into the DOD network via an email attachment or an air-gap transfer using a portable hard drive. With the right malware, an adversary can compromise personal information or the CAC credentials along with the PIN number to gain access to the Air Force network.[1]

The 2013 release of the "Air Force Social Media Guide" is a huge step in the right direction to educate users about how to use social media. Although the guide is very user-friendly, it only provides basic guidance on posting mission and personal information using social media. Foundationally, the guide provides three main themes to consider about posting information on social media platforms. The first is to encourage Airmen to tell their unique Air Force stories. Second, be honest about unit and mission without violating operations security. Finally, keep interactions conversational and informal, yet professional and tasteful.[2] All of this is a good beginning, but it fails to address the vulnerabilities of social media sites and the risk of exposing personal information online.

The following table 1 identifies the Air Force guidance evaluated for the purpose of this paper. The guidelines identified below are source referenced in the Air Force Social Media Guide or associated Air Force Instructions (AFI). Although the "Web Management and Internet Use" AFIs have been rescinded and several others have no direct social media relevance, they are included as a point of reference due to their relationship with the social media guide and cyberspace operations.

Table 1. Air Force guidance evaluated

Guidance	Status	Social Media Relevant
Air Force Social Media Guidance, 1 June 2013	Current	Yes
AFI 1-1, Air Force Culture, Change 1, 12 November 2014	Current	Yes
AFI 10-701, Operations Security (OPSEC), 8 June 2013	Current	Implied
AFI 33-129, Web Management and Internet Use	Rescinded	
AFI 33-200, Information Assurance Management, Change 2, 15 October, 2010	Current	No
AFI 33-332, The Air Force Privacy and CMI Liberties Program, 5 June 2013	Current	Implied
AFI 35-101, Public Affairs Missions, 18 August 2010	Current	No
AFI 35-107, Public Web Communications, 21 October 2009	Current	No
AFI 35-113, Internal Information, 11 March 2010	Current	Yes

The next table uses the "Air Force Social Media Guide" as a truth source to compare the AFIs addressed from the previous table. The first observation that stands out in the social media guidance under "Things to consider before posting information online," is that the member is responsible for what they post. This guidance also coincides with the public affairs AFI on internal information. The second major observation is that although gaps between the guidance and AFIs are evident, that does not mean the other AFIs are not relevant. The primary utility of this gap analysis shows what AFIs are out there and which ones may need future attention to aligning with the papers recommendations. The third observation, which is not apparent in table 2 that follows, is the AFIs do not provide any references or best practices to reduce the risks of information compromise, the vulnerabilities of cyberspace operations, or threats from bad actor activities. Overall, the primary deficiency in the guidance is that it does not connect policy, technology, and best practices. It also fails to explain the "so what" of information exposure in cyberspace.

Table 2. Gap analysis: Air Force Social Media Guide contents compared with AFIs

Air Force Social Media Guide	AFI 1-1	AFI 10-701	AFI 33-200	AFI 33-332	AFI 35-101	AFI 35-107	AFI 35-113
Things To Consider before Posting Information Online.							
You are responsible for what you post.	x			i			x
Consider how a post can be interpreted.	x						x
Maintain appropriate communications.	x						x
Social Media for Families							
Do not post exact whereabouts and activities of deployed Airmen.		i		i			
Be general about dates and locations concerning an Airman's trip.		i		i			
Do not make vacation dates public.		i					
Do not publicly post exactly how long a deployment will last.		i					
Be careful about posting children's photos, names, and schools.		i					
Be image aware.	x						i
Let children know they should seek help for cyber bullying.							
Useful Social Media Tips							
Do not post classified information.	x	i		i			x
Stay in your lane.	x						x
Obey applicable laws.	x						x
Differentiate between opinion and official information.	x						x
Use best judgment.							

Air Force Social Media Guide	AFI 1-1	AFI 10-701	AFI 33-200	AFI 33-332	AFI 35-101	AFI 35-107	AFI 35-113
Useful Social Media Tips							
Replace error with fact.							x
Be image aware.	x						x
Be cautious with information sharing.							
Avoid the offensive.	x						x
Do not violate privacy.	i						
Do not violate copyright.	i						x
Do not misuse trademarks.	i						x
Do not make endorsements.	i						x
Do not impersonate.	i						x
Do not seek personal or financial gain.							
Follow the terms of service.	i						x
x=The AFI addresses the same point as the Air Force Social Media Guidance.							
i=The AFI did not specifically address the same point as the Air Force Social Media Guidance but did have similar guidance.							

Notes

1. Dasgupta, Chatha, and Gupta, "Viral attacks on the DOD Common Access Card."
2. Air Force Public Affairs Agency, *Air Force Social Media Guide*, 3.

Chapter 5

Recommendations

Air Force personnel at all levels need to be educated on the risk of posting information on social media sites, the vulnerabilities of cyberspace, and bad actor threats. The Air Force annual information awareness training is one method to educate and update the force; however, it is not very useful as an actual reference. The following steps will shore up the guidance to close the gaps in policy, technology, and best practices and do a better job educating Airmen on the risks and vulnerabilities of cyberspace operations:

- Revise the guidelines using the framework addressed in table 3 that follows.

- Collaborate with the Department of Homeland Security (DHS) and Defense Information Systems Agency (DISA) for social media, web surfing, email, and hardware security best practices.

- Provide Air Force specific "Smart Cards" that provide easy to use information to help users configure their systems to minimize exposure to data theft or malware.

Revise the Air Force Social Media Guidance

Revise the social media guidance to address the risks and vulnerabilities of conducting social media activities on the dot mil domain and at home using personal computer networks and mobile devices. Also, as articulated by the FBI, the social media guidance needs to address the fact that any information posted on the Internet or in social media may no longer be private and that the more information posted, the more vulnerable one becomes.[1] Using the following framework of questions in table 4 as an overarching guide will act as a forcing function to ensure the revised guidance remains relevant and addresses critical areas that can put information at risk.

Table 3. Proposed framework of questions to revise the guidance

Social Media Guidance Framework
What are the risks and vulnerabilities of conducting official business and social media activities on the dot mil infrastructure and domain?
What are the risks and vulnerabilities of conducting official business and social media activities using personal hardware and devices at home and on the go?
Is the social media guidance adequate to protect the mission and the member against bad actor threats?
Are there deficiencies in guidance that may increase the user's on-line risk?
How will the Air Force surveil dangerous social media and security practices for official work on the dot mil domain, personal networks at home, and devices on the go?

Best Practices for Cyberspace Operations

Although the cyberspace landscape and technology changes at an incredible rate, there are best practices in use today by DHS that can minimize the risks of cyberspace operations. To help Americans understand the risks of being online, DHS launched a new cybersecurity awareness campaign "Stop, Think, and Connect" in 2010.[2] Another antidote to adopt for social media is "if you would not write your post, message, or email on a whiteboard in the middle of a mall for everyone to see, then don't post it or send it. It does not matter what it is." Users need to assume that all posts are public, and everyone can see them. If this principle is understood before posting information, adversaries will need to work a lot harder to find information.

Table 4 that follows is a starting point to address additional social media best practices to protect the user and their information.[3] For example, do not play social media third-party games or surveys.[4] Electing to play or participate in these surveys may be giving a third-party actor access to personal information associated with the service used to launch the application or survey. Even clicking on innocuous web links from a social media platform is risky behavior. Devices can be infected with malware to exploit social media network accounts or take control of the computer.[5] Also, care should be taken with any third-party applications added to one's profile. There is no guarantee that these applications have been reviewed or officially approved by the social media network and may contain malicious code. The best way to avoid becoming a victim is to understand the risks and consequences.

Table 4. Best practices

Social Media
Minimize the amount of and type of information you post
Verify all 'friend' or 'connection' requests verbally or face-to-face
Keep profiles private and limit what information 'friends' and 'public' can see
Do not post any information that would compromise yourself, your family, or the mission
Do not use the same passwords on multiple social media profiles
Keep all social media security settings set to "high"
Do not give the same access to all groups such as friends, family, or other lists
Do not play third-party games or participate in surveys found on social media platforms
Use extreme caution when adding third-party applications to your profile

Table 5 that follows is a starting point to address key areas of concern that should be included in the best practices to educate and inform Airmen.[6] These include web surfing, email, and hardware best practices. For example, when surfing the web, verify or validate all links and file downloads before executing. If the link says "www.hotmail.com" but changes to something else when you place the cursor over the hyperlink, this is a good indication that the link is redirecting you somewhere else and that you should not click on it. If on a mobile device and the link cannot be validated, do not click on it. As another example, turn off the "auto connect wireless and connections to an unsecured network" function on mobile devices—this also applies to Bluetooth connections. If this setting is turned on, an unsecured internet café location or bad actor can auto connect to the device secretly.[7] These are by no means a complete list of best practices; however, it addresses some of the most common mistakes people make in cyberspace. To date, there's no single Air Force repository of information online where a user can go that addresses the issues raised in this paper.

Table 5. Best practices

Web Surfing
Do not surf unfamiliar territory in cyberspace
Verify or validate any web links or file downloads before executing or opening
Before you click on a web link, make sure the destination URL is the same as the embedded link
Never click and open unsolicited messages or pop-up windows when browsing the internet
Email
Use purpose-specific throw-away email accounts for unimportant information and to control spam
Do not download or open attachments until you know they are safe
Do not use the same passwords on multiple email accounts
Delete any spam email claiming that it will fix your computer, social media accounts, or financial access
Hardware
Hardware and software updates and patching should be automatic, frequent, and transparent
Review the privacy statement and permissions the program wants to access before installation
Use strong passwords of at least ten characters that contain letters, numbers, symbols
Use credible security and virus protection on all of your computer devices
Use reputable antivirus and firewall software that automatically scans and updates as needed
Do not store anything you want to protect on any device that connects to the internet

Air Force Smart Cards

Another way to educate and inform Airmen and their families would be to post informational smart cards that go over the basics on how to best configure social media accounts. The FBI created four "Social Media Smart Configuration Cards" that the public can download for use to cover how to configure accounts.[8] As part of Canada's education after a recent shooting of its troops, they provided their members with similar social media smart cards to update the configuration of their social media accounts; see note for details.[9] The Air National Guard's 115 Fighter Wing also posted a set of social media smart cards to help users configure their accounts.[10] The Air Force should collaborate with DHS and DISA to create Air Force specific Smart Card solutions as part of an ongoing user awareness campaign. The development of Smart Cards that address web surfing, email, and hardware best practices is recommended to go one step further. Full-page examples of the smart cards in figure 6 below are located in Appendix 1 for reference.

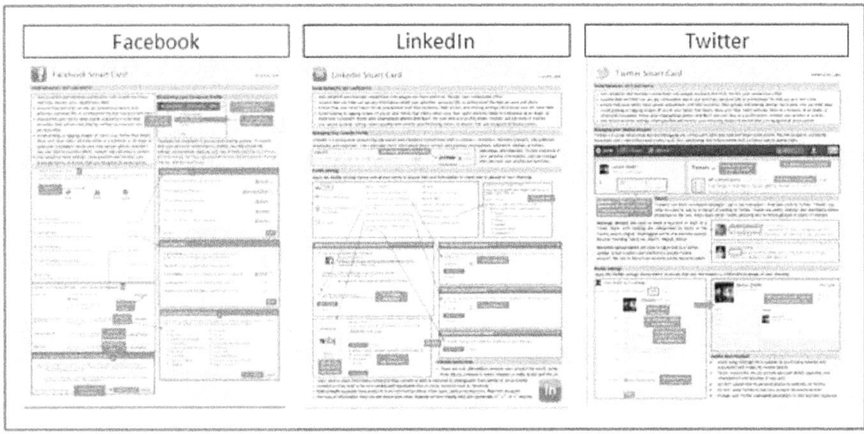

Figure 6. FBI social media smart cards

Notes

1. Federal Bureau of Investigations (FBI), "Internet Social Networking Risks."
2. Department of Homeland Security, "Stop, Think, Connect."
3. AFOSI, *AFOSI Special Product*; FBI, "Internet Social Networking Risks"; and Oxley, "Best Practices Guide."
4. Oxley, "Best Practices Guide."
5. FBI, "Internet Social Networking Risks."
6. Aucsmith, Senior Director, Microsoft Cyber Security, "Cyber Security"; Oxley, "Best Practices Guide"; and FBI, "Internet Social Networking Risks."
7. FBI, "Internet Social Networking Risks."
8. FBI, "Social Media Smart Configuration Cards."
9. Authors Note: On 24 October 2014, two days after a reservist guarding the National War Memorial in Ottawa was shot dead, the Canadian Forces Counter Intelligence Unit issued a new directive regarding social media practices to its soldiers and staff. The new directive asks members of its National Defense Staff and Armed Forces to remove any photographs of military personnel in uniform or reference to their employment from social media profiles. Coorsh, "Military Gets New Social Media Policy in Wake of Attacks."
10. 115 Fighter Wing, "Smart Cards."

Chapter 6

Conclusion

Airmen and their families are the Air Force's essential and finite resource. However, if they are in a position where they cannot accomplish the mission, they become a liability. Reckless social media practices and cyberspace operations can put the individual or mission at risk or in a compromising position. Even without being reckless, sensitive personal information is at risk if the person or organization becomes a target of opportunity. Individual users need to understand that they are accountable for their actions in cyberspace. Most users do not understand the connection between a single reckless post or wrong mouse click and the consequences it can create down the road for the mission, the member's information, or the devices they are using to interact with the internet.

The FBI's key recommendation for self-protection and for protecting the mission is to reduce one's online footprint and presence to minimize the vulnerability of compromising personal information.[1] It is important to understand that no matter how well personal data is protected, friends and family may not be as security conscious. In turn, personal information like contacts and text messages that reside on computer systems can be compromised and put personal information at risk. However, even with the best security practices and software, systems compromised with malware or lost or stolen mobile devices still risk compromising any data stored on the system or mobile device. Ultimately, protecting personal information has less to do with how to use the technology, but more to do with what the technology can reveal about what has been posted, emailed, or searched for in cyberspace.

Revised social media guidance and the use of smart cards can help close the user education gaps between policy, technology, and best practices for cyberspace operations. All of the recommendations addressed in the paper can be implemented using existing resources and partnership with DHS and other DOD organizations with minimal cost to the Air Force. Whether the end product is new guidance or updating the current guidance, it needs to address the risks and vulnerabilities of web surfing, email, and hardware security to educate the users better and close the gaps between policy, technology, and best practices. Additionally, developing Air Force specific smart cards on social media, web surfing, email, and hardware security would be an invaluable quick reference aid that can educate users on smart cyberspace operations while reducing the risk of information exposure or malware infections. In conclusion, an educated and informed workforce can better protect the Air Force mission and decrease the danger of becoming a target of opportunity for foreign adversaries or criminal actors.

Notes

1. Federal Bureau of Investigations, "Internet Social Networking Risks."

Acronyms

AFI	Air Force Instructions
BYOD	Bring Your Own Device
DHS	Department of Homeland Security
DISA	Defense Information Systems Agency
DOD	Department of Defense
EXIF	exchangeable image file format
FBI	Federal Bureau of Investigation
ISIS	Islamic State of Iraq and Syria

Appendix

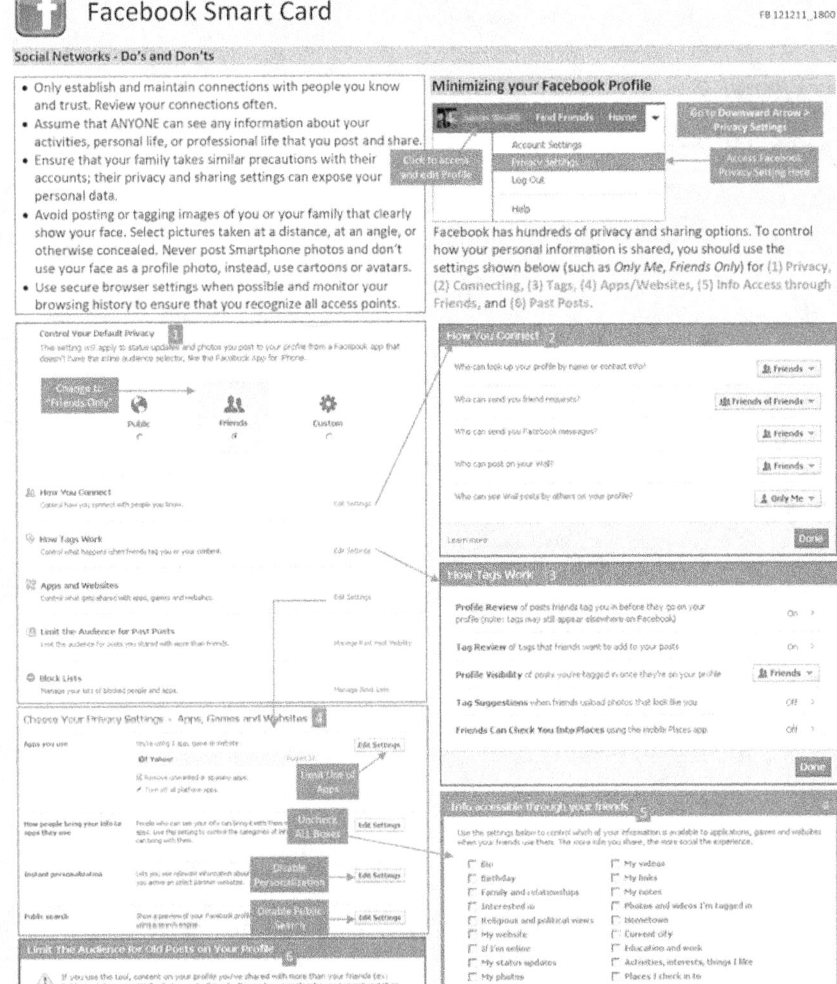

Facebook Smart Card
FB 121211_1800

Social Networks - Do's and Don'ts

• Only establish and maintain connections with people you know and trust. Review your connections often.
• Assume that ANYONE can see any information about your activities, personal life, or professional life that you post and share.
• Ensure that your family takes similar precautions with their accounts; their privacy and sharing settings can expose your personal data.
• Avoid posting or tagging images of you or your family that clearly show your face. Select pictures taken at a distance, at an angle, or otherwise concealed. Never post Smartphone photos and don't use your face as a profile photo, instead, use cartoons or avatars.
• Use secure browser settings when possible and monitor your browsing history to ensure that you recognize all access points.

Minimizing your Facebook Profile

Go to Downward Arrow > Privacy Settings
Account Settings
Privacy Settings
Log Out
Help

Click to access and edit Profile
Access Facebook Privacy Setting Here

Facebook has hundreds of privacy and sharing options. To control how your personal information is shared, you should use the settings shown below (such as Only Me, Friends Only) for (1) Privacy, (2) Connecting, (3) Tags, (4) Apps/Websites, (5) Info Access through Friends, and (6) Past Posts.

 **Facebook Smart Card**

FB 121211_1800

Do not login to or link third-party sites (e.g. twitter, bing) using your Facebook account. "Facebook Connect" shares your information, and your friends' information, with third party sites that may aggregate and misuse personal information. Also, use as few apps as possible. Apps such as Farmville access and share your personal data.

Profile Settings

Apply and save the **Profile** settings shown below to ensure that your information is visible to only people of your choosing.

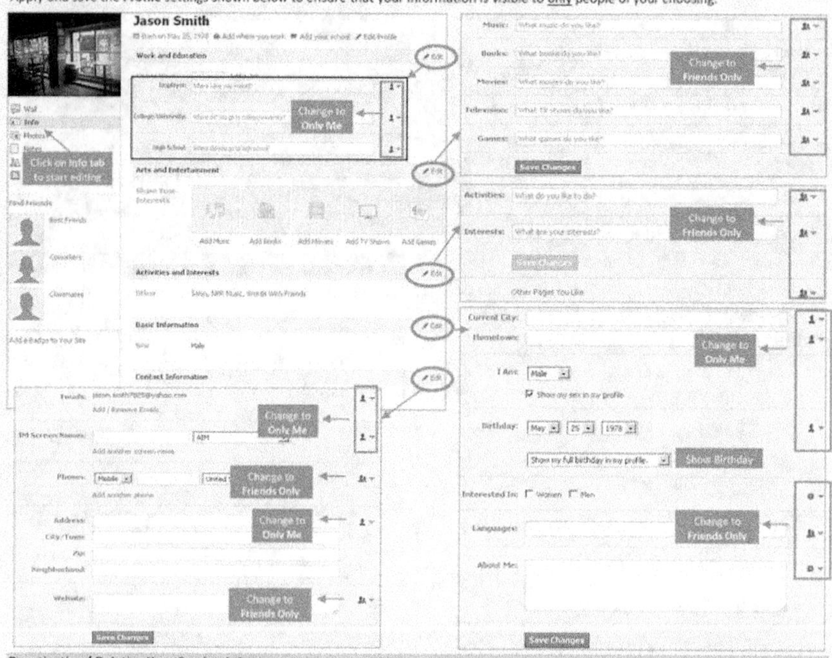

Deactivating / Deleting Your Facebook Account

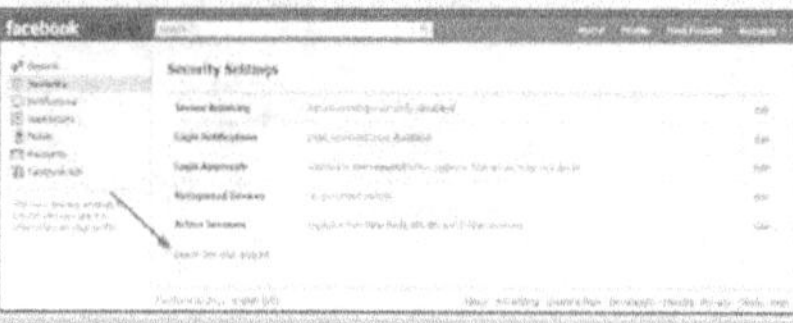

To **deactivate your Facebook account**, go to **Account Settings** and select **Security**. To reactivate your account log in to Facebook with your email address and password.

To **delete your Facebook account**, go to **Help Center** from the account menu. Type **Delete** into the search box. Select **How do I permanently delete my account** then scroll down to submit your request here. Verify that you want to delete your account. Click **Submit**. FB will remove your data after 14 days post security check.

Useful Links

A Parent's Guide to Internet Safety	www.fbi.gov/stats-services/publications/parent-guide
Wired Kids	www.wiredkids.org/
Microsoft Safety & Security	www.microsoft.com/security/online-privacy/social-networking.aspx
OnGuard Online	www.onguardonline.gov/topics/social-networking-sites.aspx

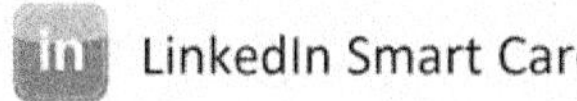

LinkedIn Smart Card

Social Networks -Do's and Don'ts

- Only establish and maintain connections with people you know and trust. Review your connections often.
- Assume that ANYONE can see any information about your activities, personal life, or professional life that you post and share.
- Ensure that your family takes similar precautions with their accounts; their privacy and sharing settings can expose your personal data.
- Avoid posting or tagging images of you or your family that clearly show your face. Select pictures taken at a distance, at an angle, or otherwise concealed. **Never post Smartphone photos and don't** use your face as a profile photo, instead, use cartoons or avatars.
- Use secure browser settings when possible and monitor your browsing history to ensure that you recognize all access points.

Managing Your LinkedIn Profile

LinkedIn is a professional networking site whose users establish connections with co-workers, customers, business contacts, and potential employees and employers. Users post and share information about current and previous employment, education, military activities, specialties, and interests. To limit exposure of your personal information, you can manage who can view your profile and activities.

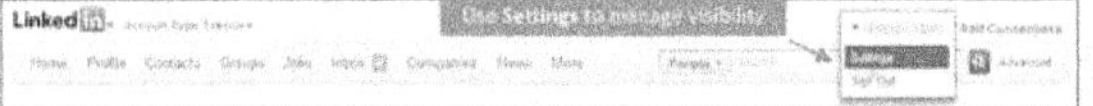

Profile Settings

Apply the **Profile** settings shown with arrows below to ensure that your information is visible only to people of your choosing.

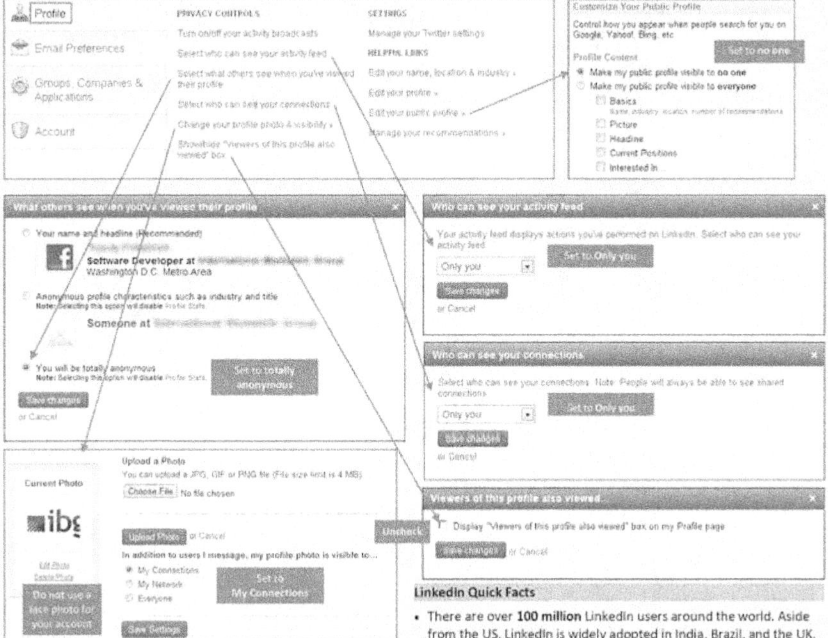

LinkedIn Quick Facts

- There are over **100 million** LinkedIn users around the world. Aside from the US, LinkedIn is widely adopted in India, Brazil, and the UK.
- Users tend to share information related to their **careers or jobs** as opposed to photographs from parties or social events.
- LinkedIn profiles tend to be more **visible and searchable** than in social networks such as Facebook.
- **Paid LinkedIn accounts** have access to more information about other users, such as connections, than free accounts.
- The type of information users can see about each other depends on how **closely they are connected** (1st, 2nd, or 3rd degree).

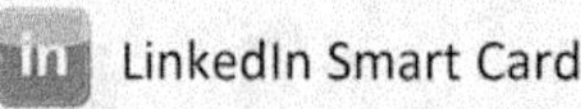# LinkedIn Smart Card

Account Settings

Apply the Account settings shown with arrows below to ensure that your information is shared in a limited fashion.

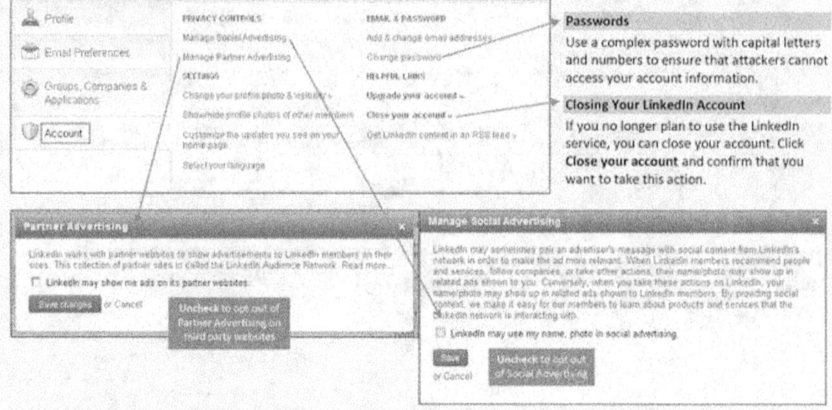

Passwords

Use a complex password with capital letters and numbers to ensure that attackers cannot access your account information.

Closing Your LinkedIn Account

If you no longer plan to use the LinkedIn service, you can close your account. Click **Close your account** and confirm that you want to take this action.

Application Settings

Third-party applications and services can access most of your personal information once you grant them permission. You should limit your use of applications to ensure that third parties cannot collect, share, or misuse your personal information. Apply the **Application** setting shown with arrows below to ensure that your information is visible only to people of your choosing.

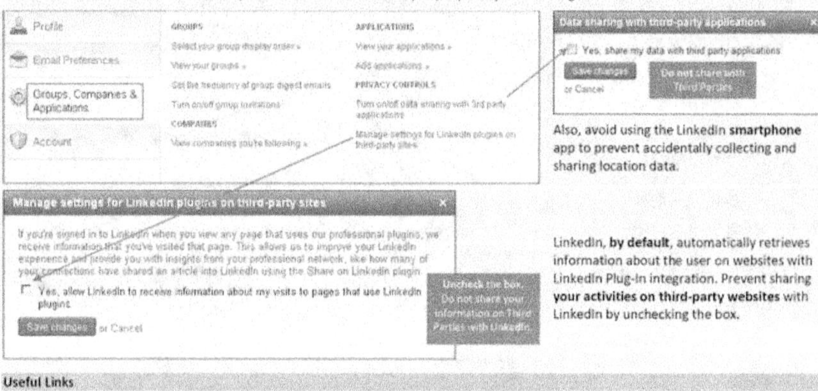

Also, avoid using the LinkedIn **smartphone** app to prevent accidentally collecting and sharing location data.

LinkedIn, **by default**, automatically retrieves information about the user on websites with LinkedIn Plug-In integration. Prevent sharing **your activities on third-party websites** with LinkedIn by unchecking the box.

Useful Links

A Parent's Guide to Internet Safety	www.fbi.gov/stats-services/publications/parent-guide
Wired Kids	www.wiredkids.org/
Microsoft Safety & Security	www.microsoft.com/security/online-privacy/social-networking.aspx
OnGuard Online	www.onguardonline.gov/topics/social-networking-sites.aspx

Social Networks -Do's and Don'ts

- Only establish and maintain connections with people you know and trust. Review your connections often.
- Assume that ANYONE can see any information about your activities, personal life, or professional life that you post and share.
- Ensure that your family takes similar precautions with their accounts; their privacy and sharing settings can expose your personal data.
- Avoid posting or tagging images of you or your family that clearly show your face. Select pictures taken at a distance, at an angle, or otherwise concealed. **Never post Smartphone photos and don't** use your face as a profile photo, instead, use cartoons or avatars.
- Use secure browser settings when possible and monitor your browsing history to ensure that you recognize all access points.

Managing your Twitter Account

Twitter is a social networking and microblogging site whose users send and read text-based posts online. The site surged to worldwide popularity with +300 million active users as of 2011, generating 300 million tweets and 1.6 billion search queries daily.

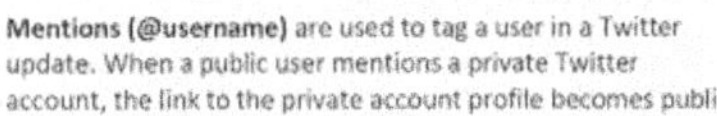

Tweets

"Tweets" are short text-based messages – up to 140 characters – that users post to Twitter. "Tweet" can refer to a post as well or to the act of posting to Twitter. Tweets are public, indexed, and searchable unless protected by the user. Many users never Tweet, choosing only to follow persons or topics of interest.

Hashtags (#topic) are used to mark a keyword or topic in a Tweet. Posts with hashtag are categorized by topics in the Twitter search engine. Hashtagged words that become popular become Trending Topics (ex. #jan25, #egypt, #sxsw).

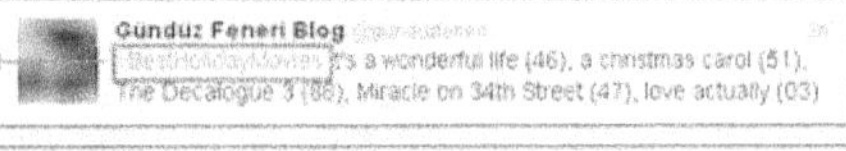

Mentions (@username) are used to tag a user in a Twitter update. When a public user mentions a private Twitter account, the link to the private account profile becomes public.

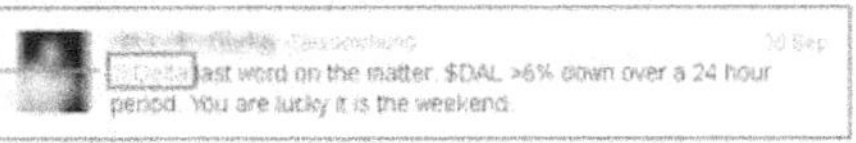

Profile Settings

Apply the **Profile** settings shown below to ensure that your information is visible only to people of your choosing.

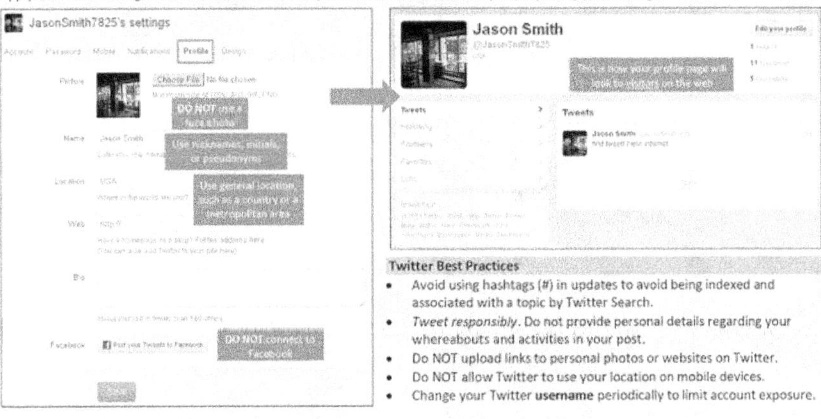

Twitter Best Practices

- Avoid using hashtags (#) in updates to avoid being indexed and associated with a topic by Twitter Search.
- *Tweet responsibly.* Do not provide personal details regarding your whereabouts and activities in your post.
- Do NOT upload links to personal photos or websites on Twitter.
- Do NOT allow Twitter to use your location on mobile devices.
- Change your Twitter **username** periodically to limit account exposure.

 # Twitter Smart Card

Account Settings

Apply the **Account** settings shown below to ensure that your information is shared in a limited fashion.

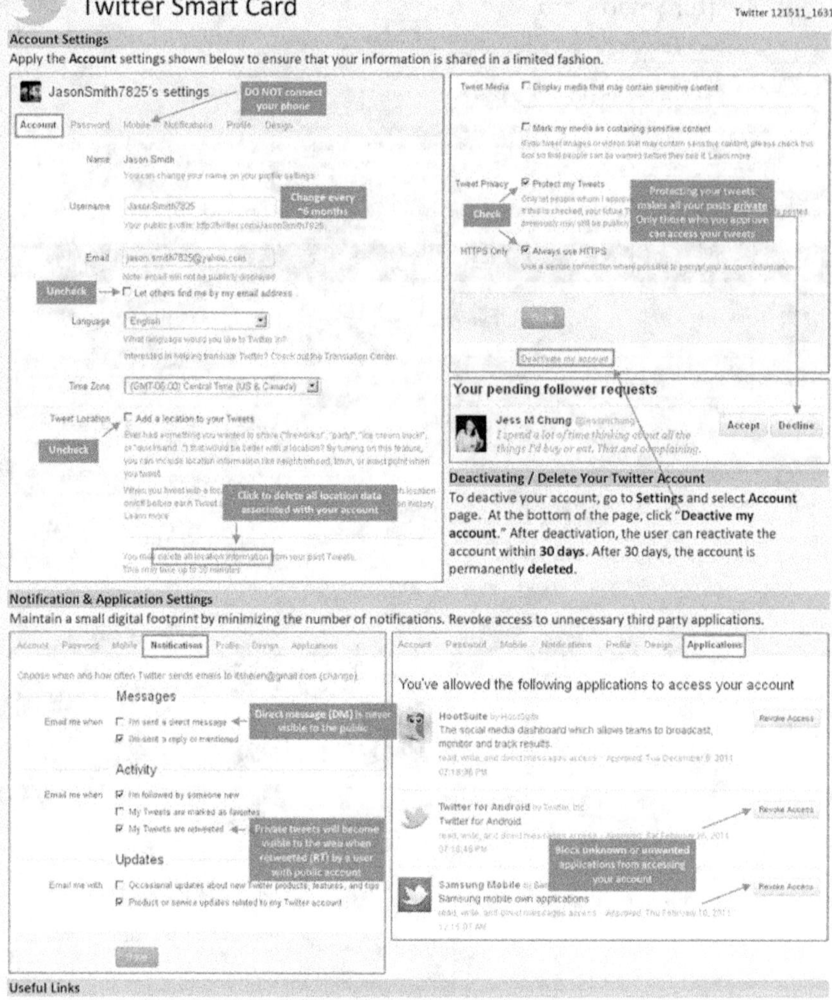

Deactivating / Delete Your Twitter Account

To deactive your account, go to **Settings** and select **Account** page. At the bottom of the page, click "**Deactive my account.**" After deactivation, the user can reactivate the account within **30 days**. After 30 days, the account is permanently **deleted**.

Notification & Application Settings

Maintain a small digital footprint by minimizing the number of notifications. Revoke access to unnecessary third party applications.

Useful Links

A Parent's Guide to Internet Safety	www.fbi.gov/stats-services/publications/parent-guide
Wired Kids	www.wiredkids.org/
Microsoft Safety & Security	www.microsoft.com/security/online-privacy/social-networking.aspx
OnGuard Online	www.onguardonline.gov/topics/social-networking-sites.aspx

Bibliography

Air Force Instruction 1-1. Air Force Culture, 7 August 2012 with change 1, 12 November 2014.

Air Force Instruction 10-701. Operations Security (OPSEC), 8 June 2011.

Air Force Instruction 33-200. Information Assurance Management, 23 December 2008 with change 2, 15 October 2010.

Air Force Instruction 33-332. The Air Force Privacy and Civil Liberties Program, 5 June 2013.

Air Force Instruction 35-107. Public Web Communications, 21 October 2009.

Air Force Instruction 35-101. Public Affairs Missions, 18 August 2010.

Air Force Instruction 35-113. Internal Information, 11 March 2010

Air Force Policy Directive 33-2. Information Assurance (IA) Program, 3 August 2011.

Air Force Public Affairs Agency. *Air Force Social Media Guide*, 1 June 2013.

Air Force Office of Special Investigations (AFOSI). *AFOSI Special Product: Safeguarding USAF Personnel's Online Presence* (U). CENTCOM.mil, 10 September 2014. Unclassified, For Official Use Only. https://www6.centcom.mil/WelcomeGuide/WelcomeGuideFiles/CENTCOM%20Information/Cyber%20Security%20Information/Safeguarding%20service%20members%20Online.pdf.

Alexander, James. "Maltego Connection Mapping." Jalexander-WMF at English Wikipedia, 31 August 2015. https://commons.wikimedia.org/wiki/File:OrangeMoody-BubbleGraphCombined-Nolabels.jpg.

Aucsmith, David, Senior Director, Microsoft Cyber Security. "Cyber Security." Lecture, Air University, Maxwell AFB, AL, 1 November 2014.

Boone, Jason. "Criminal Use of Social Media." National White Collar Crime Center Research Associate, 2013. http://www.iacpsocialmedia.org/Portals/1/documents/External/NW3CArticle.pdf.

Bradbury, Danny. "In Plain View: Open Source Intelligence." *Computer Fraud and* Security, April 2011, 5–9. http://www.sciencedirect.com/science/journal/13613723/2011/4.

———. "Data Mining with Linkedin." *Computer Fraud and Security*, October 2011, 5–8. http://www.sciencedirect.com/science/article/pii/S1361372311701014.

Brown, Pamela, and Jim Sciutto. "FBI Warn Military of ISIS Threat." *CNN*, 1 December 2014. http://www.cnn.com/2014/12/01/politics/fbi-warns-military-of-isis-threat/.

Coorsh, Karolyn. "Military Gets New Social Media Policy in Wake of Attacks." CTVNews.ca, 24 October 2014. http://www.ctvnews.ca/canada/military-gets-new-social-media-policy-in-wake-of-attacks-1.2070490.

Dasgupta, Partha, Karmvir Chatha, and Sandeep Gupta. "Viral attacks on the DOD Common Access Card (CAC)." Tempe, AZ: Department of Computer Science and Engineering, Arizona State University, N. D. http://cactus.eas.asu.edu/partha/Papers-PDF/2007/milcom.pdf.

Department of Homeland Security. "Stop Think Connect." http://www.dhs.gov/stopthinkconnect (accessed 29 January 2015).

Duggan, Maeve, Nicole Ellison, Cliff Lampe, Amanda Lenhart, and Mary Madden. "Social Media Update 2014." Pew Research Center, 9 January 2015. http://www.pewinternet.org/2015/01/09/social-media-update-2014/.

Ernst and Young Global, Limited. "Bring Your Own Device: Security and Risk Considerations for Your Mobile Device Program." EY.com, September 2013. http://www.ey.com/Publication/vwLUAssets/EY_-_Bring_your_own_device:_mobile_security_and_risk/$FILE/Bring_your_own_device.pdf

Federal Bureau of Investigations (FBI). "Internet Social Networking Risks." FBI. http://www.fbi.gov/about-us/investigate/counterintelligence/internet-social-networking-risks (accessed 13 October 2014).

———. "Social Media Smart Configuration Cards." FBI. http://www.etsu.edu/oit/helpdesk/smcards.aspx (Accessed 4 November 2014).

Goodchild, Joan. "Social Media Risks: The Basics." *Networkworld*, 3 Feb 2010. http://www.networkworld.com/article/2243920/collaboration-social/social-media-risks--the-basics.html.

———. "5 Facebook, Twitter Scams to Avoid." *Networkworld*, 13 July 2009. http://www.csoonline.com/article/2124183/social-networking-security/5-facebook--twitter-scams-to-avoid.html.

———. "Social Media Risks: The Basics." Networkworld, 31 August 2009. http://www.csoonline.com/article/2124305/security-awareness/5-more-facebook--twitter-scams-to-avoid.html.

Gonsalves, Antone. "Eight tips for More Secure Mobile Shopping." CSOOnline.com, 3 December 2013. http://www.csoonline.com/article/2134197/mobile-security/eight-tips-for-more-secure-mobile-shopping.html.

Hatchimonji, Grant. "Why Giving Mobile Apps Banking Info Isn't as Risky as It Seems." CSO.com.au, 8 September 2014. http://www.cso.com.au/article/554514/why-giving-mobile-apps-banking-info-isn-t-risky-it-seems/.

Herridge, Catherine. "Source: Air Force father, Son Targeted Online by ISIS Followers." FoxNews.com, 7 October 2014. http://www.foxnews.com/politics/2014/10/07/source-air-force-father-son-targeted-online-isis/.

Healey, Jason. *A Fierce Domain: Conflict in Cyberspace, 1986 to 2012*. London: Carbon Capture and Storage Association, 2013.

Higgins, Kelly J. "30,000 Machines Infected in Targeted Attack on Saudi Aramco." DarkReading.com, 27 August 2012. http://www.darkreading.com/attacks-breaches/30000-machines-infected-in-targeted-attack-on-saudi-aramco/d/d-id/1138287.

Jones, Jeffrey M. "About One in Four U.S. Households Victimized by Crime." Gallup.com, 5 November 2014. http://www.gallup.com/poll/179174/one-four-households-victimized-crime.aspx?version=print.

Mallery, John R. "Computer Forensics: More Places To Look—Social Networking @ Cell Phone Evidence." BKD Forensics Institute. http://www.bkd.com/services/forensics-investigation-litigation.htm (accessed 4 November 2014).

M-Trends: Beyond the Breach: Mandiant Annual Threat Report—2014. Mandiant: A FireEye Company. https://www.mandiant.com/resources/mandiant-reports/ (accessed 12 October 2014).

Madden, Mary. "Public Perceptions of Privacy and Security in the Post-Snowden Era." Pew Research Center, 12 November 2014. http://www.pewinternet.org/2014/11/12/public-privacy-perceptions/.

Murtagh, Rebecca. "Mobile Now Exceeds PC: The Biggest Shift since the Internet Began." *Search Engine Watch*, 8 July 2014. http://searchengine-watch.com/sew/opinion/2353616/mobile-now-exceeds-pc-the-biggest-shift-since-the-internet-began#.

Opanda. "PowerExif Editor." Opanda.com. http://www.opanda.com/en/pe/ (assessed 12 January 2015).

Oman, Hilarie. "The Morris Worm: A Fifteen-Year Perspective." IEE Security and Privacy 1, no 5 (2003): 34-43. https://www.computer.org/web/csdl/index/-/csdl/mags/sp/2003/05/j5035.pdf.

115 Fighter Wing (FW), Air National Guard. "Social Media Smart Cards." 115 FW. http://www.115fw.ang.af.mil/shared/media/document/AFD-120605-029.pdf (accessed 4 November 2014).

Oxley, Alan. "A Best Practices Guide for Mitigating Risk in the Use of Social Media." IBM Center for The Business of Government. http://observgo.uquebec.ca/observgo/fichiers/71490_RiskUseofSocialmedia.pdf (accessed 12 October 2014).

Paterva. "Maltego Software." Paterva.com. https://www.paterva.com/web6/products/maltego.php (accessed 12 January, 2015).

Pun, Ray. "Adobe 2013 Mobile Consumer Survey: 71% of People Use Mobile to Access Social Media." Adobe, 25 July 2013. http://blogs.adobe.com/

digitalmarketing/mobile/adobe-2013-mobile-consumer-survey-71-of-people-use-mobile-to-access-social-media/.

Reynolds, Karen. "Good Technology Supports Air Force Mobile Device Operational Capability." Good.com, 3 April 2013. http://www1.good.com/about/press-releases/201115161.html.

Schelihaas, Kristine. "Are Your Facebook Posts Compromising Military Security?" *Military 1*, 20 April 2014. http://www.military1.com/army/article/461049-are-your-facebook-posts-compromising-military-security.

Schanz, Marc V. "Hard Looks at Growing Missions." *AF Magazine*, January 2012: 22–24.

Thomann, Andreas. "Skype—A Baltic Success Story," Credit-Suisse.com, 6 September 2006. https://www.credit-suisse.com/us/en/articles/articles/news-and-expertise/2006/09/en/skype-a-baltic-success-story.html.

White House. "Bring Your Own Device: A Toolkit to Support Federal Agencies Implementing Bring Your Own Device (BYOD) Programs." *Digital Government*, 23 August 2012. https://www.whitehouse.gov/digitalgov/bring-your-own-device.

Williams, Brett. "Cyberspace: What Is It, Where Is It and Who Cares." *Armed Forces Journal*, 13 March 2014. http://www.armedforcesjournal.com/cyberspace-what-is-it-where-is-it-and-who-cares/.

Winnefeld, ADM James A., Jr.,Vice Chairman of the Joint Chiefs of Staff. "Ends, Ways, Means, and National Interests." Lecture, Air University, Maxwell AFB, 2 October 2014.

Yannakogeorgos, Panayotis A., and Adam B. Lowther, eds. *Conflict and Cooperation in Cyberspace*. Boca Raton, FL: Taylor and Francis Group, 2014.